Dying for Beginners

Patrick L. Clary

LOST BORDERS PRESS

BIG PINE, CALIFORNIA

Lost Borders Press
P.O. Box 55
Big Pine, CA 93513
e-mail: meredith@lostborderspress.com
www.lostborderspress.com

LOST BORDERS PRESS and colophon are registered trademarks
of The School of Lost Borders.

Library of Congress Cataloging-in-Publication Data

Clary, Patrick, 1950–

Dying for beginners

cm.

ISBN 0-9777632-0-x $15.95

1. Poetry; 2. Death and dying; 3. Ecopsychology;
4. Literary commentary

CIP

Designed by Sarah Felchlin
Cover photograph by Patrick Clary

First Edition
Manufactured in USA

ACKNOWLEDGMENTS

Poems have appeared in The Bulletin of the American Academy of Hospice and Palliative Medicine, CoEvolution Quarterly, Dryad, Journal of the American Medical Association, Journal of Medical Humanities, Journal of Palliative Medicine, New England Journal of Medicine, Patient Care, Saxifrage, Three Sisters, and Windows

A number of these poems also appeared in a chapbook, *Notes for a Loveletter*, published by Washington Writers Publishing House

For

Mary Beth Rhiel

and

Joseph Durocher

CONTENTS

Foreword

Introduction

DEATH VALLEY VISION FAST   1

MY FATHER AND MY MOTHER   3

WAITING SUPPER SOUTH OF FALLON   4

MAKING CONNECTIONS   5

WAR STORIES   6

ORIENTATION AT BIEN HOA   9

ROVING AMBUSH   12

WAR'S A JOKE   13

LAMENT FOR VO VANH THOM   14

THE ROLLER COASTER   16

NEW TESTAMENT   18

NOTES FOR A LOVELETTER   19

NOTHING SURPRISES YOUR TRUE INTELLECTUAL   23

THE FUNCTION OF MODERN POETRY   24

DAYS I DON'T REMEMBER   27

THE SAXOPHONE   28

GUSTAV MAHLER IN AMSTERDAM, 1910   30

THE TRANSLATOR   32

THREE VARIATIONS   35

WINTER IN BUCKS COUNTY   40

THE MISTAKE   41

PATIENT   43

LONG DISTANCE   44

THE WATCH   45

A JIG FOR MY WAKE   46

I Find My Friends 47

The Woman Who Loves the 18TH Century 48

Elegy for Robert Chamberlain 50

Dear Monica 52

Parable of the Bad Shepherd 54

The First Year My Earnings Will Exceed
My Father's 57

ICU 58

Xmas in Brooklyn, 1982 59

Epithalamion 61

The Pain 62

Learning the Language 66

Eating Leftovers on Nantucket 68

The Sound of Air Over Wings 70

Five Tasks Taught by Hospice Nurses 72

Meditation Lesson in the *Pays d'Oc* 74

Millennium Fire 75

Three from Upaya Zen Center 76

Grief Work 77

Dying for Beginners 78

Memorial Day 80

Afterword: Origins of the Earwax Patrol 83

FOREWORD

The title poem, "Dying for Beginners" opens with
this stanza:

> *Our chaplain's sixtieth birthday present to himself*
> *was the new career he saw on a vision-fast in the*
>   *canyon lands.*
> *He would help others over the river, as harbor seals*
> *are said to help lost swimmers, nudging them*
>   *toward shore —*
> *practice for mortality by serving other mortals.*

These lines announce the burden of Patrick Clary's
work—an introduction to dying by way of hospice
work. Help to the dying acts as preparation for death.
Clary himself did a vision-fast in Death Valley, and
prepared for it by spending a day on Mt. Kearsarge in
New Hampshire, when the park was closed for winter;
the author climbed to the top in the snow. He is an
adventurer of the body and of the spirit. When he
was young, his spiritual eclecticism could take him
into danger. In "Bad Shepherd" he writes about an
encounter with Peoples Temple before the mass suicide
in Guyana: *Jim Jones was the only man I ever met whose*
face gave off light. These qualities of risk and adventure
inform his poems.

    The "Acknowledgements" are unusual for such
a collection: *Journal of the American Medical Association,*
Journal of Palliative Medicine, New England Journal of

Medicine... The author is indeed a medical doctor, like Keats or William Carlos Williams, in our own day and age when it is rare to find a poet who is anything but a poet, usually attached to an English Department. Offhand, I do not think of another profession—not insurance executive, not vice-president of General Foods—more conducive to poetry than medicine, with its burden of love and death. I am taken with how Clary's poetry, when its manifest content is nothing medical, reaches into the profession for its images: *She has the eyes of a child waking after general anesthesia... she ties words/One-handed into surgeons' knots.* These lines come from a poem called "The Woman Who Loves the 18th Century." It is firmly not about medicine, but about the woman, with the poet's occupation supplying the word-horde.

In this collection we see Patrick Clary's active and many-sided life. Clary is a Quaker and during the Vietnam War was a conscientious objector who served as an infantry medic in the field. His Vietnam year enters many poems here, savage in their realism and pointed toward the event of death, at which we are all personal beginners.

Coming back from that battlefield, Clary took an AB in English, working especially on poetry with the poet Roland Flint, then went on to medical school and for most of his life has practiced family medicine. Gradually he has become more and more devoted to attendance upon the dying. He left family medicine entirely to assume a more prominent place in his region's hospice movement. He has visited medical schools to teach issues in the care of the dying which might otherwise go unexamined, speaking all over the country to those who will attend patients at the ends of their lives. The titles of some of his dozens of lectures and papers give a sense of Clary's scope: "Healing the Healer: Poetry in Palliative Care," "Breaking Bad News," "Last Hours of Living," "Wellness at the End of Life," and "The Art of Dying." One essay, "Building a Better Deathbed," names the place that Clary has come to. Ninety percent of people, when they die, he tells us, die predictably rather than suddenly. "For most of this vast majority, death could occur at home surrounded by family, in comfort, with appropriate support. This is what…most Americans want at the end of their lives. Instead, more than three-quarters of us die in institutions. Half of those who die in hospitals and eighty percent who die in nursing homes die in pain. This is worse than a national disaster; it is something like an ongoing, if unintentional, holocaust." Clary has become, as he calls it, "a practical Buddhist." Years ago, the daily meditation practice meant to support the spiritual life of a family doctor revealed a persistent small voice that urged him toward more hospice work. Wherever he teaches about difficult issues in the care of the dying, "it seems useful to have a place for eyes to rest. A dozen yellow roses in a clear glass vase on a green tablecloth are a favorite focal point, off to my left – the heart side." This is for the eyes of the palliative care worker, not for the dying but for the helper who accompanies the dying.

My favorite poem here is called "The Pain," a brave and frightening monologue. Here we find the dense recollections of a radical doctor who by his profession encounters pain regularly. He starts by talking about a drunk:

> *There is a man*
> *stinking of blood, oil and beer waiting for*
> *another pair of hands in the emergency room*
> *and he cannot stop screaming...*

and moves to other extremes:

> *I have touched, gently as the antennae of a roach,*
> *a violated two-year-old who screamed at everything,*
> *even her own hands groping toward tattered flesh.*
> *I have diagnosed gonorrhea in nonchalant*
> *   four-year-olds...*

Clary is impatient with any passivity in the face of pain, and most of all with ignorance and indifference to the dying. This book ends with a marvelous medical story. A woman in a nursing home, silent and uncaring, appears to be succumbing to Alzheimer's, even to approach her death. In the prose anecdote, "The Origins of the Earwax Patrol," Clary tells how in his examination he found both ears clogged by hard earwax. He describes the long struggle, by varying treatments, to remove the wax down to the drum—and how with hearing restored the woman stopped showing symptoms of advancing dementia and other morbidities. She began listening again, she talked, and she lived in the fair health of old age for several years.

This story shows the practical doctor dealing with something as mundane as earwax. Patrick Clary, his compassion combined with fierce attention, *sees* the dying and schools his own center to make each beginner's journey into death as gentle as may be. Quaker, Buddhist, Vision Quester, he has condensed his diverse experiences into a book of poetry suitable for mortals, or anybody who loves them.

– Donald Hall

INTRODUCTION

In our frenetic, clangorous times, a book of poetry might seem like an artifact from a bygone era: ethereal, antiquated, surely impractical. People once read poetry to learn how to live, and I suppose it would be naïve to suggest that contemporary poetry, too, might possess the power to instruct, or guide, or inspire. I will do so anyway, and recommend Patrick Clary's *Dying for Beginners* as Exhibit A. Emotionally weighty and eminently readable, this book is impractical and antiquated only if you can think of no current use for the art of empathy.

The poems collected here span a period of about thirty-five years, roughly the duration of my friendship with the author, which began in a poetry workshop at Georgetown University in 1974. I was a nineteen-year-old junior; Patrick was slightly older than the rest of us, having made a life-changing detour to Vietnam, where he served as a medic bearing witness to daily murder, his coming of age forever contaminated by the gore and violence and stupidity and repetition and futility of war. Though the physically imposing young poet who landed in our sunny second-floor classroom had apparently returned from the war in one piece, you could almost hear him shatter as he walked, and in those days he had a penchant for knocking into things, as if his grief and rage took up invisible space beyond his corporeal borders. Our teacher, Roland Flint, a deceptively jovial fellow, took poetry as seriously as any warrior ever took war. Roland was the first person I ever knew who lived by poetry. Patrick became the second. Under Roland's tutelage, Patrick wrote ten times as many poems as the rest of us that year, a furious output that launched a lifelong mission of fashioning a whole, fully inhabited life out of his wrecked pieces. *Dying for Beginners* is the story of that life.

Throughout much of the book's first half, the poet-narrator speaks in the voice of a cynical, soul-crushed medic wrestling with a war, and a subsequent homecoming, marked by loss, bewilderment, and fury. *Count me among the / Angry grotesques of a small bar,* he calls to us in "New Testament." In "Three Variations," we hear strains of the medic's swagger as he keeps vigil over a dying relationship: *Sometimes I want to be the scar / In your hand which will interrupt / Your life...* Later, we meet the same poet in different guises—medical student, intern, resident—but the echo of war haunts these middle poems, too. *When I left the hospital tonight / Just before visiting hours began / The seasonal platoon of stuffed animals / Already stood guard at the entrance,* he recounts in "Xmas in Brooklyn, 1982," a poem written on the battlefield of inner-city health care. *There are no toy stores among those miles / Of tenements rocked blind, burned, then abandoned / As if the next war had come early but couldn't stay.* The medic persists—still ministering to the dying, still at war, still stymied by languages he can't speak, lives he can't fix, institutions he can't humanize. He interprets his own pain by examining, sometimes intensifying, and only occasionally releasing the pain of others. And yet, like nuggets of gold in a muddy streambed, poems of a different material turn up during this somber period: glimmering love letters, elegies, poems to beloved friends. The bonds of language begin to loosen as the poet stumbles toward beliefs that can be expressed only through his poetry. *Love is inevitable, silent as water— / If we are patient it will come to us,* he writes to a bridal couple. To a dead friend he proclaims, in admiration and forgiveness, *You did everything well except living forever.*

By the time we find the poet in middle age, a family doctor with a family of his own, the book makes a final, gratifying shift: the poet's life has ceased to unravel and begins instead to unfold. In "Eating Leftovers on Nantucket," the poet revels in food and family by baking a cake—*twice from scratch / To get it right*—with his young niece. *...and the family eats / Every crumb of both golden cakes.* At the end of the book, in "Memorial Day," the poet returns to the West, simultaneously mourning his father and brother and celebrating his sons. *Catch and release is the story of my life, of all our lives,* he tells us. He is fishing the Lamprey River, a place that recalls the spiritual and geographical territory of his youth, and in this remarkable poem a lifelong search for purpose transforms itself, through the medium of poetry, into a search for meaning.

As I read Patrick's poems now, especially those I remember hearing him declaim in the weekly readings we lived for back in college, I do not hear *his* voice, but *a* voice—a cry from, and for, the universal *us.* For, despite his moments of tender admission, Patrick Clary is no poet of confession; he tells his singular story by packing the poems with other people—their stories, their voices, their blessed wounds. In this he proffers the old and valuable literary gift of paradox, abundant throughout. The poems beckon us to silence as they give voice to what might fill that silence. They whisk us away from the teeming world by lighting our way back into that same world. They answer the questions we never thought to ask, and question the answers we never thought to doubt. And they end with beginning.

Yesterday I spent the evening at Patrick's home in the company of his wife, his young daughter, and one of his grown sons. We had beautiful food. Some music. Singing. Talk of poetry. Outside the snow fell and fell, while my old friend settled into his well-lighted parlor, surrounded by loved ones. Who ever could guess the origin of this happy arrival? Patrick is a poet-physician now, a national leader in the field of palliative care, once again embracing the dying in a full circle too exquisitely drawn to be accidental. He teaches end-of-life-care to practitioners through poetry; he brings poems into sickrooms as if they were flowers. And though he is far too busy to write letters, he still writes me regularly, as he has for the past thirty years, a letter a month or more in exchange for mine. When he moved to New Hampshire, a mere 52 miles from my doorstep in Maine, our correspondence took scant notice of the convenience, for it is through letters that we have maintained our long friendship and explored the themes that inform our writing: loss, politics, family, literature, work, love. In his letters I often find poems in the making: an observation about a friend or patient, a report of a tragedy or celebration, words set down with care and intention, words that call for a return of that same care. This is how one maintains friendship with a real poet, by inhabiting a realm where poetry is not something one writes, but something one lives.

I invite you to enter this realm, to befriend this compassionate veteran of the deathwatch as he recounts a long, perilous journey from observer to interpreter to believer. *Now I see: living is a kind of slow burning,/ And love is what we salvage from the fire.* Here, now, in the year 2006, I invite you to practice the timeless art of learning through poetry, beginning with a book of poems penned by a man who himself is still learning.

— Monica Wood

DEATH VALLEY VISION QUEST

Folded basalt thrusts into the blue shield of sky.
F-18s thunder through briefly,
Playing at war over the Funeral Mountains.
A web of bright contrails spreads higher than ravens can fly.

Sparse creosote and desert holly,
Like a Vegas showgirl's negligee,
Emphasize geology rather than concealing it:
Noonday Dolomite bled from hot depths,
Then weathered in a million years of rain;
A marble canyon sculpted smooth as young skin;
Slopes of shattered rock find their angle of repose,
But slide underfoot;
Alluvial fans point to rivers
That flow only every other year.

In the silence the warplanes leave
I can hear my own heart again,
Beating out the orders that drove me to this wilderness
To fast and rehearse my death.
A human heart stops forever every second somewhere,
Someone stepping through that door
Into another unexpected beginning,
Or a very dark and silent heaven.
Even rehearsal can be terrifying:
It seems dying well takes practice.

I thought I would simply live
Until I succumbed to the punishments of time.
Today the raven who knows my mother's maiden name
Showed me the way up Mount Forgiveness,
Stones shaped by slow rain into a vertical bed of nails,
Every two-sided spike a betrayal.
These lacerations have not been penalties,
But the accidental, sharp edges of the world,
Opening me up.
                                        Suddenly,
I find all my wounds are turning into blessings.

MY FATHER AND MY MOTHER

My father said it was a blessing
For a man like him who never talked much
Or listened to much music
To have a woman singing in the kitchen.

My mother said it was a blessing
To have my father there to listen
When he was starved for music,
To be the music in his life.

My father and my mother say it was a
Blessing when I arrived, late as always,
To grow like a wish in my mother's songs.

Though I know she sang those lullabies to me,
She left the door ajar so he could hear,
A man in love who made a woman sing.

WAITING SUPPER SOUTH OF FALLON

By dust that snakes toward home again
The dry-eyed women know their men
Return. In this there's no routine
Of counted hours. Nevada green
Is only torn from thankless tasks
Away down dirt-road miles. The masks
The women wear are faces lost
To drought and bars and days that cost
What weeks and months might once have paid.
They say, "Come in, wash up, the table's laid."

MAKING CONNECTIONS

Between Kansas
And California
The roads are so empty,
Buses run always
On time.

In Las Vegas, Nevada,
At the Greyhound station,
Two women share a bench
And shuffle snapshots
Of each other's grandchildren.

I look out at the littered
Pavements of morning.

I am the grandson of a man
Who died alone here
In the Clark County Hospital.

WAR STORIES

I.

We were waiting for assignments in Texas after being trained as medics. Because I outranked the rest by one stripe, our cadre sergeant put me in charge of the paint detail. I stationed one man outside with a bucket and brush to keep watch while the rest of us played eight-ball in the cadre dayroom. Johnson and I got our orders for Vietnam the same day. I asked him what he was looking for on the large wall map hung next to the cue rack. "'Nam," he answered, without turning his head, as his finger traced the course of the Mississippi.

II.

In a short time the new medic and the new second platoon leader had become close friends. When we moved they would march close together in order to talk. Of course the platoon leader's two radiomen had to stay close to him as well. I thought the four men in parentheses of antennae made a fine target. The Vietnamese peasant who emptied the magazine of his AK into them late one afternoon must have agreed with me. He couldn't resist so we got him too. The bodies were a full return load for that evening's supply chopper. When we returned to Firebase Libby three days later a Spec 5 from the battalion aid station told me they had thought I was dead. "That was Larsen," I said. I always marched among the riflemen of the third platoon, distinguished only by my lack of such a weapon.

III.

Framed by the firing slit a flight of Phantoms napalmed a jungle hillside the telescopic rangefinder said was five klics away. It was near sunset and visibility was perfect. I had never seen a more beautiful landscape. Sad and Clarkson sat on either side of me in the dark bunker, waiting their turn with the 'scope and drinking warm beer. Dapplin' Dan was already lying enveloped in his hammock comfortably smoking thick joints of two-dollar marijuana. A replacement stuck his head in the door and asked where he could report to the platoon sergeant. I told him. Then he said, "Hey, you guys, what's that smell? Something's burning in here you guys." Clarkson nodded at the swaying hammock: "'S only Dapplin'," he said.

IV.

Military intelligence learned that a pregnant woman of the local VC cadre was going into labor out in a jungle base camp. She would either have to be brought into the ville or a midwife would have to go out to her soon, along with a shipment of supplies for the rest of them. My platoon set up as far as possible from the trail they would be most likely to use in either case. We stayed up all night, drinking grape Kool-Aid from olive-drab canteens and sending in the routine negative sitreps of an unsuccessful ambush.

V.

The pain of Fivekiller's wounds astonished him both times. Morphine calmed him right down during the long wait for the Medevac helicopter. A month later he came back to the field, walking point and limping a little. He gave up smoking. He wanted never again to feel real pain, he said, and he heard lung cancer could be incredibly painful. Just after I left the platoon they surprised a North Vietnamese rifleman who shot Fivekiller several times through the chest. He still looked surprised when I visited him in the 34th Evacuation Hospital weeks later.

ORIENTATION AT BIEN HOA

I. ORDNANCE

White phosphorous is not for use
On targets, only for marking purposes,
The Geneva Convention says,
And the regulations say,
Like they told you at Fort Benning.

Call for an airburst on a grid —
Counting seconds flash-to-bang,
And that ball of cotton hanging in the sky
Will tell you where you're at,
Like they told you at Fort Polk.

But I'll tell you if you're in shit —
Men falling in the storm of steel rain
From a thunderhead of forest —
Twenty marking rounds of Wilson Pickett
    on the deck'll
Make a cloud nothing can come out of.
It marks them up pretty good I can tell you
Like they didn't tell you at Polk or Benning.

I smelled them burning.

II. WITH A SMILE

Yes, gentlemen,
This little war here
Exists only
For one reason:

To give you all the pleasure
You can handle.
Why we got a service
Worked out
Where any time you want
We can have a smiling
Oriental with an AK pop up
And tear you out
A brand new asshole
Sometimes you don't even have to ask.

III. THE CEREMONY

I'm here to tell
You this here
M 16 E-1 rifle, assault,
Good for two things.

One is, if it don't jam,
If you keep it clean enough
But not too clean,
Put eighteen holes in

Whatever you point it at
Inside of two seconds.
And if whatever you point it at
Is a gook, and it don't jam,
You just ruined his whole day.

Two is, if you can hunt up a bayonet,
Be the centerpiece
In a touching ceremony
 – along with one pair of spit-shined boots
And a steel pot from supply –
Like you saw in some war movie
With Mr. John Wayne,
And this is supposedly supposed
To improve company morale
After Charlie jump dead in your shit
And knock over some
Replacement you never knew
Name or line number of,
Who's standing up,
Yelling,
"Why'd you all fall down
So Goddamn quick?"

ROVING AMBUSH

Rollers of white dust
Wash the coastal plain
In this season of no rain.

Our trails are nets of tripwires we must
Cut but see first to cut:
Monofilament fish lines lead to Chicom claymores,
Stolen baseball grenades in opened mackerel cans, pins
Pulled, handles ready to fly, and daisy cutters in pools
    of rice straw.

We are almost gone,
Tantalized by daily rumors of evacuation and retreat.
Maps published in Paris in '58
Show rubber plantations now dense with brush;
Buddhist graveyards sit where
Villages should be.

We pay in blood for targets and see
No field of fire, nothing for the fee,
This seeping body bag, strapped
For carrying between four men,
An Atlanta grave as yet unmapped.
Out of water, I borrowed a canteen,
Paying with a promise: I'll visit *your* grave
Bring fresh flowers, and a memory of
How other times we turned warm Asian flesh to cold
As our rhythmic weapons rocked and rolled.

WAR'S A JOKE

See, it was odds
Of twenty to
One
Scared shitless
The whole firefight
Got off one clip
Lowcrawling the
Goddam hill with these crazy
Motherfuckers'
Riflefire cutting the trees
Into trash and toothpicks
But we got him
We got that sucker
Twenty to
One,
Us or him.

LAMENT FOR VO VANH THOM

If you can smile while they cut off
Your right hand with a bayonet they
Have only used to open ration cans,
You will weep when you lose your son.

There will be no scar,
But when you are hungry
There will be nothing to carry
The rice to your mouth.

We were never hungry among the rats
And dogs of the firebase dump,
As the soldiers threw away
More food than they ate,

And guarded these riches
Carelessly. The guards had nothing
Behind their eyes and nothing
In the magazines of their rifles.

We knew to eat what the rats ate,
And thought the silver sand
Leaking unmolested from gnawed bags
Was only poison —

Until today one of the guards
Smiled to himself, lit a
Cigarette and threw the match
Into the shining dune.

Meters away my hands burned, my son screamed.
When they wrapped my hands in white cloth
While my son lay gasping without medicine
In the wet shroud of his skin,

I knew there was no reason to follow.
Though now they lay on the floor
Of the gray Chinook together,
The man with the match would be alive in
America tomorrow, my child dead in Da Lat.

THE ROLLER-COASTER

The first thing I always remember is the roller-coaster.
Later I learned to talk again.
In a short time I would find myself married.
Most of us never saw each other again.
We promised to write and didn't.

There was a lot not to say.
My little brother stopped asking and followed
    me everywhere.
He did not understand the philosophy of
    concealment or
The blunt weapon of silence.
Even his blue eyes would not have saved him.

I took a color photograph of all 28 members of
    my platoon
Early one evening.
My shadow and the shadow of the camera
    leaned awkwardly
Over Clarkson's shoulder. Their faces were masks.
The sky burned through their eyes
Onto the film in my camera.
Only the black soldiers did not accuse me.
Their eyes on the earth, they were shadows like
    my shadow,
Strangers, and survivors. All the soft-eyed white
    boys were already gone.
Later, in an ambush, even blue-eyed Clarkson died.

In my first memory, my brother is still just
Young enough to hold my hand as we walk toward
    the roller-coaster
Over the beach at Santa Cruz.
Becky is there with us, her hair floats
To the faint swell of her hips.

She has waited like Penelope and I have not returned.
Instead she finds lame strangers claiming her
Armed only with silence.
I would slay these suitors if they were not mute,
If I did not understand them to be fragments
    of my life.

She told me often, in letters, how she longs
To ride this roller-coaster through clouds of seabirds
With me until our hearts stumble over each other
In terror and joy. I buy a hundred tickets.

After three runs she will refuse to ride again.
She will watch as Mike and I ride through the gulls
Until the sun is our blood-trail West on the water.

NEW TESTAMENT

Count me among the
Angry grotesques of a small bar.
There is a small man
Reading next morning's
Post at my elbow who wants to touch me.
There is a fat cook with no
Prospects ironing a white
Shirt in the kitchen
And the beaked face of the
Bartender is sucking up
Cigarettes and beer while he
Dies of emphysema
And wonders if his numbers hit.
"Give me the sports page,
George. 'Skins lost again."
Count me among the ones
Who don't count, can't count
And never will.
Count me among the angry
Grotesques of a small bar.

NOTES FOR A LOVELETTER

I love you but it's so difficult to stop writing.
　　　　　　　　　　　　– Kenneth Koch

The monster selling gum on the bus
Is not walking down the aisle on his knees
He has no knees
And no need to kneel while
He can walk on half
His missing
Legs there is no stopping him
His shoes are boots on backwards his

Two hands are claws
He had a bad accident
He was born
He can't remember
But his body won't forget
For a moment neither will we
He is not supposed to be here
Selling gum on the bus
Only the children are buying
He counts back a girl's change as if he were
A woman not in love
But reluctant to admit it
I have a need to kneel
I am reluctant to admit to men in beige

Three-piece suits
Women in mauve gowns and white

Who address the ball
With ebony mallets
At the foot of the lawn
In my mind as I write
Buttercups fleck the green slope with sunlight
    children gather
Twilight and though it is effortless
I cannot stop it

For we are not in this century
I do not know where we are

Five old men shelved on a bench like
The bestsellers of 1954 are asking why survive
Pitying the young who must Harry
Is burying automatic weapons
In his backyard Harry says his heart's not in
It he has two kids and they have more
Things are going to get bad
Then get worse Harry says
Interesting like the
Chinese curse
If they took over at least we
Could walk the neighborhood at night
The young are going to survive
That's about it
Harry still has connections in the
Army and offers me a piece
Harry the connection I made in the army was
I couldn't survive killing anybody
I'm your civilized and suicidal intellectual

Harry smiles
Knowing I have a
Shotgun in my closet
Leftover from my own war
The magazine unblocked to hold

Six illegal rounds
Every spring we thought about shotguns
The bartender said
An old friend taking a break
At my table in Mr. Smith's Garden
But we're not zoned for shotguns
The pigeons were so bad
We had to do something
We sent away for a tape of ravens
Killing rock doves and it works real well
Even turned down low
The pigeons leave the old ladies
Drinking and eating the free popcorn alone
Every once in a while though
When I come in for a morning shift
I find a bird dead in the popcorn machine

Seven sins have become my face
A thing like a raven
That sits on my shoulder eating
The pigeon trapped in my chest
Dickie don't stare at the man
His pets are his own business
Mommy it's so hard to stop
Raven

Ate my body a bloody battleground
I carry on I read
All of Shakespeare
O glaube, mein Herz, o glaube,

Nein, ich liess mich nicht abweisen
No, not even after the world
Becomes Kansas the heart
Will not stop
There is no stopping it
Even after the military rites out of an old
Series of degradation and departure
After being broken to
Private
Given a sentence of hard labor
A couple of sets of fatigues
And bound in barbed wire
The heart continues
To issue painful orders
Out of radio contact
Out of food
Weaponless
Whole armies of children mutiny
Through the dark forests

Ten movements of obsession and conceit
Is my heart
In these words
I cannot stop

NOTHING SURPRISES
YOUR TRUE INTELLECTUAL

for Gerry Pecht

Your true intellectual
Thinks most of the time.
There are thirty-six hundred
Seconds in an hour.

It takes an hour to walk to
Work across Key Bridge from Georgetown
With a six-pack in the afternoon,
Dropping empties into the Potomac.

Which means either "River of
Swans," or "Trading Place," depending
Upon who you put
The question to.

There are no swans and few
Indians here now, there is nothing much
Here now but plastic
Palaces and echoing halls

And a hotel where zonked clerks
Play chess alone while Senators seduce interns.
It doesn't take much.
It takes nothing to surprise your true intellectual.

THE FUNCTION OF MODERN POETRY

Believe it or not as you read this
You are remembering a beggar on a bus
In Washington DC one warm winter day
When the snow was melting as it fell
And kept falling metaphysically
This is simply the way words work
Saying no to your life by giving you
Memories you never had

Do you remember the Diane Arbus photograph
"Boy with Toy Hand Grenade"
Lady that hand grenade's no toy just as your
Leica is no toy you can see he's going
To kill you in three seconds you stopped him
There forever

Remember that when I speak of memory
I am being metaphysical things on the
Edge of not existing are metaphysical
Poetry
A service station attendant smoking a cigar
My conscience
The famous "man with the rubber chicken"
Who sits above the penalty box and goes
Berserk at every hockey game then
Goes home in time for the late news
Becomes metaphysical for a moment when
He says to the wife "that's me on the tube"

But he's probably right as the
Tao Te Ching has probably been
Right all along
The Way is not this, the
Way is not that, the
Way is not this or that
The Way is unspeakable
Which is all a
Way of saying
Some things endure
Some things last longer than others
And the last thing is that
Which comes closest to nothing at all
Things like water we disregard
Deliberately or ignore
This is not what the Tao is saying
The Tao is saying nothing

In this country poetry lasts a long time
Poetry the disregarded
Memory of something that never happened

Like a character actor the virtues
Poetry has are mainly negative
Poetry is proudest of the things it has said no to
To priests to musicians to the sincere and
The virtuous to good lovers and happy men

Poetry says yes to drunks
Suicides
Blind men and the

Vice Presidents
In charge of
Bilking widows and orphans
Those whose lives say no every minute
From the center of pain
In the city of self-indulgence

Some things last longer than others
I swore the words forever once
I was married in a red shirt
I still have the shirt

DAYS I DON'T REMEMBER

There are days when I don't remember you,
Not the good days, not the bad days,
Just days I don't remember.

Lately the sky has opened for nothing
But the rain. Like you, everyone is
Closed to me. We talk of nothing but the weather.

This is the season when loons
Land on the night roads
Mistaking them for rivers,

To tangle wings like women's legs
In the shattered windshields
Of speeding cars.

There was a time when words seemed to be my wings.
Now they only weight my heavy body,
And all my roads are turning into rivers.

THE SAXOPHONE

for Alan Altimont

I am listening to the recorded voice
of a man talking plainly,
almost as if to himself,
saying how difficult it is
to get the news from home.
He has been dead many years.
The dead man's son says
when Ezra Pound visited Rutherford
he took over everything. It was
"Polish my toenails! Bring me a drink!"
Dad was upstairs, intoxicated
Spouting happy genius, polishing a poem.

"Let Ezra drape himself all over everything like a fat
housecat. We just got him out of the madhouse!
I stopped listening to him anyway
except when he told me to write.
You could never tell what language he was speaking
Or even whether he spoke it."

Sometimes Williams must have thought about
        madness too,
Writing poetry everywhere, on prescription pads,
in patient records, even in books.
Think of a man doing three things at once:
Family, medicine, poetry, producing,
as his son says, a continuous draft,

typing until two in the morning, up again
at five to write a letter to old Ezra,
wherever *he* was, Italy, England;
hating Eliot across a whole ocean,
corresponding with 200 literary magazines,
delivering kids – "That Jones!
Helluva big baby!" – Jesus Christ!

I myself, listening to this impossible old man
on the radio saying many poems I love, think of
my closest friend, who hesitated,
piling his instruments into the back seat
of his rattletrap Subaru in an empty parking lot:
hesitating in a parking lot,
far below the anatomy labs where I was supposed
    to be studying,
and shrugging, Italian as Corleone,
and taking the saxophone case out again,
and the gold sax out, and playing
first a scale of quarter notes, then a long glad
skirl of bop to nobody, nobody he knew was listening
(but to me it sounded like the news from home).

GUSTAV MAHLER IN AMSTERDAM, 1910

Alma, I will not write this letter. I do not know what the weather was when I arrived. The great physician who has consented to become my friend berates me with your youth and my inexperience, then speaks enigmatically of the spring. I know it is not spring here. You are in the South. Is your architect of the sanitarium there with you? I ask Freud what he finds at Leyden to holiday at such a place. He spins riddles of glass and vision, and of the spring. He is more a poet than a physician, telling me, in this dead August, that flowers are the songs trees sing. Each tree, blossoming, seeks to become the future just as words seek to become poems and poems seek to become the silent harmony of understanding. My mind has not been harmonious since we counted out the losses you have suffered in our marriage. Your dead songs, you say, follow you like a coffin. We are both bereft, and I am old now.

Once, I told you that we might finally find our home here, where they first understood my Seventh. Last night three musicians listened to that song of the earth I nearly called, in spite of my superstition, the Ninth Symphony. I am afraid to excuse them by observing that the piano was not well tuned. When I told them the title of the work, the concert-master of their Philharmonic laughed, and complained facetiously of seasickness, asking, to more laughter from the others, "When are we going to get back on the dry land of this song?" I did not continue to play, ending with part of the melody of the second movement.

In his wandering enigmas my great friend has supplied me with words to contradict that tuneless laughter. They say that this song of the earth sounds like the sea, and they are correct. The earth longs to become the sea. The sea, in Freud's riddle, is the song of the earth. I am told, I believe in Asia, and the west coasts of the Americas, the earth does move most violently at intervals, and at such instants the earth seems to be like the sea, and it sings, in the lowest notes, such a song as the sea sings in the higher. Singing is only a soul's breath moving the ether. We all want to become higher beings: the stone wants to become the fertile earth, the earth longs for the moving rivers, the rivers seek the seas, and the seas seek to move the air; and who has not heard the sea, even in the least likely places as in the rain and wind in the trees of the Tyrol? My friend has explained my dreams to me in the same terms of longing.

Indeed, there are other longings: the tree in flowering seeks to become the future, just as we did through our own children. I have gathered these longings together like flowers into music. There are those elements which satisfy their longings. The rock wears away into earth, the earth washes away into rivers, and the rivers find the sea, and who has not heard the music of the sea, even in the wind and rain? But no one among all the living knows his children will become the future. Dear Alma, my songs are our children, they will be understood. In the future, lovers may think of us when the trees flower.

THE TRANSLATOR

There must be fifty ways to leave your lover,
Fifty ways to leave your lover.
– Paul Simon

Imagine that I am the Dominican who
Just put all his coins into the cigarette machine
That doesn't work in the drugstore on the corner
Of Thirtieth and P and I stand there staring
And I say in desperation
I don't speak English
I don't speak English

Imagine that we kept a
Tape recorder going all
The years we were together
Freezing every word and silence
I've begun listening and I find
The tapes are in some language
I do not understand

That's not an excuse which would
Have occurred to me
As the things that are more or less
True never *occur*
Never happen in time
But arrive too late and use force
Like the *Guardia Civil*
Who do not really care

Whether you speak their language or not
They speak yours

That silence moving through our lives was me

Once you said in the bar at Keflavik
"You must know eleven languages
Well enough to order two beers"
And I took it as a compliment
But you didn't mean it

Imagine me in the basement with seventy miles
    of tape
At 3 ¾ i.p.s. dubbing desperately
Over my silences
Giggling, humming, pretending I was there
Ordering beer in Spanish, Russian, Vietnamese,
And not meaning it not making sense

Imagine me not making sense
The night I finally told you to leave
I knew without leaving
How many ways there are to leave your lover —
I used them all: silence, the friends
Neither of us liked, poetry,
The drinking, places I had to be
Things I had to do
Finally, silent,
You just left.

Imagine that you never woke me to
Kiss me goodbye that Friday morning
Imagine that I had noticed that
You had removed my
Grandmother's rings to place them in an envelope
Inside my expired passport
With my birth certificate and DD-214
In the bottom drawer.

Imagine me returning from Philadelphia
    Sunday night
And not finding that all your books
Were gone from our shelves and that our bed
Was an empty shelf

Even the fact that I had
No excuse was an excuse
Beneath my words the tape holds only silence

I hear myself on new tapes now
Telling other women what I should have told you
Nothing comes out
I don't speak English
I don't speak English

THREE VARIATIONS

I. The Hands

I remember sitting with Annie
At the ballet as she translated
Chopin into a language
Her deaf children could understand.
I wanted to be in love then, too.
It is surprising, but not unpleasant,
To be reminded of something so
Long forgotten. Now, unexpectedly,
You remind me of Annie, you remind
Me of that music, your hands bring the dancing
Language of the deaf into my silent life.
Your hands too, as you speak,
Play the invisible instruments of silence.
I think of my grandmother's hands,
And the piano she can no longer play
And the endless crocheting
Of afghans now lying on beds, on couches
In drawers everywhere, every grandchild
Finally satisfied. I think of my
Grandmother's hands resting.
I think of my own hands, square,
Filled with themselves, professionally
Tender on demand, but still uneasy
At your easy tenderness. I think of
Your hands, beautiful as a promise,
The hands I thought all women's hands
Might be when I was ten, hands large with

Tenderness, full of innocent caresses,
Wearing grace like silver rings.
Your hands are the hands of the woman
Who has not yet taken up permanent
Residence in your body, the woman
We each see once, across a street in the rain,
Across a river, across ten years of time,
Across anything unbridgeable,
The woman you promise not because
You care but because I remember,
I see her in your hands,
And I hope for her,
As Annie's children hoped for music.

II. Breakfast Poem

It is raining. You are
Playing your flute
Down muffled scales,
Each note the sounding
Of a temple bell shrouded in burlap.
I have never heard anything
So like the rain.

You are the ghost we would all
Love, the one I always almost meet,
The girl with the violin I almost
Speak to on the bus.
Too slow, propelled only by longing,
I fall in love with your shadow
And it is your stop.

You remind me of the year I brought
Valentines to my fourth grade class
On the wrong day. I was in love then too.

It is strange, though. Here you are.
Your hands are cold. So are your feet.
You love me. I am all you need
In a man. But there are conditions.
You don't need a man very much.
You can live with your cold feet.
Sometime in the near future
There is a break in your life line.
You are leaving forever. You hope to live
On prayer, then nothing. Disembodied,
You promise you will visit.
I swear never to have an unlisted number.
I promise you a poem for breakfast.

It is nearly winter. Falling leaves,
Like your body, make the wind visible.
Sometimes I want to be the scar
In your hand which will interrupt
Your life, and sometimes I do not.
Sometimes I want only to begin to know you
After you have passed some difficult
And unconditional surrender to the possible,
My need translated into your
Vertical language of mirrors.

The rain becomes snow, and
Disappointed crows cry. A squirrel

Chatters in his nude tree
Like an old man surprised bathing.
Do not interrupt the poem of your
Body with such foolish modesty. I am familiar
With the anatomy of farewells.
You are leaving, and I will not ask you
Not to leave, I will only
Ask that you return when
You can no longer live alone in the
Cold of your long journey, when your feet must carry
You back to the fire we made of our bodies,
When your hands must hold onto me, when
At last you can speak to me in the language of bells
And I can answer, when, finally, we will be
In transit together, travelers in a country
Where breakfast, and poems,
Are always late, but on time.

III. Letter to an Institution

It is raining at night when I dream.
You are here again, playing your flute like the rain.
We live in a fortress of glass
Defended by soldiers with no hands,
Besieged by a white-uniformed army of physicians.
The army waits for my orders in the rain
And my soldiers wait for their hands.
I dream of an answer.
No one asks: they only stand and wait. I dream
      all night
Of death and wake to a world in which death

Falls like rain, a world in which I wear a white coat
And write orders for palliatives and placebos.
Nothing is curable. I cannot help these people
Beating themselves to death with their fists,
Stabbing themselves with knives.
Even if I run out into the rain screaming
They will continue to make plans for their pain
And my own, inventing and contracting new diseases,
Giving birth to strangers, plotting to be shot
By the police. In my dreams I am the
Surgeon General, I operate brilliantly
On all these injurious hands. My soldiers are birds,
I have given them wings, they are beautiful.
For myself I have only these dreams.
You could write and tell me why your mind snapped,
Why you tuned to the high notes of screams and bells.
Then you would be real. Then I could pretend
    you exist.
Are only angels and the mad beautiful?
You told me once I was beautiful in my sleep.

WINTER IN BUCKS COUNTY

The last leaves and the last rain had fallen
And the low forest had frozen into a maze of glass.
That was another country then,
Far from your father's house across the road.

There you could skate through the cold music
Of woodland, snowfall, and heartbeat.
Ice blossomed among the roots
And the trees held night in their arms
As mothers hold children.

Blood was your new language;
Still, you danced over the flawed mirrors of ice
On steel wings, your speed a matter of balance
And sway as if even gravity had become a friend.

Nothing is that easy now. But if your forest is lost,
You carry its music through the city with your grace
And only you blame those who love you for listening.

THE MISTAKE

Five years we have lived in this city
Without hurting each other.
It would be a mistake to talk to you now.

I remember a poetry reading after a cold morning
On a day the sun began promising summer.
You carried the long burgundy coat we bought
For you in Paris with the last of our money.
You left after I read and asked only that
I carry the coat home in the car; I forgot.
Since leaving me you have generally avoided poetry.
I have avoided other places, other things:
The zoo where a friend saw you once, our friends.

Those who are my friends now never knew you,
Except Richard, who still asks after you, and
Has a letter you wrote he never answered.
Matthew, who saw you feeding the elephants,
Moved to Ohio. I ran into Fig once on the Hill
Then never saw him again. When I was in
San Francisco this summer I called your
Father's office but found he'd moved to Reno
Three years ago. Annie is in Guyana.
Last year I thought I saw you at a poetry reading,
Though I was mistaken. Funny that you were there.

I met one of our old friends at a party
Last week after, what, three years?
I explained why I couldn't see her again.
She claimed she never sees you and hit me twice, hard,
Before I could get my motorcycle started.

It has been five years. Still, this morning at breakfast
I found myself reading your horoscope out loud, half
That old morning ritual we made of the friendly and
Ambiguous advice next to the funny papers.
You are still half the census of all my dreams.
No one reads my horoscope to me now smiling
        as you did.
I miss you. I no longer want not to miss you.
I am leaving Washington in the spring.
I don't want to see you, or love you, or hurt you.
This poem is a mistake.

PATIENT

Old men belted into wheelchairs
White nurses,
Cries behind green doors
Are nothing
To this black child
Singing a nursery rhyme
In the emergency room.

LONG DISTANCE

You call collect from New York
You expected me to be there
You tell me to come up anytime when
I arrive you
Will be somewhere else you
Are always somewhere else when
You were here I had
Keys made I would have given you my own
You refused them you
Said you'd rather call first you
Feel more comfortable
I promised to stay here all night
All the doors were open
The second night you stayed with me the
Phone rang and we
Let it ring
I froze for an instant though
I thought it might be you

THE WATCH

These hands are praying only to themselves.
Every day ticks like a bomb.
Instead of exploding it disappears.
Friends, lovers, their hearts ticking,
Go off and become strangers.

I too have become a stranger.
I wake screaming, in my own bed,
In my own room, holding my own hands.

Once clocks and desire ordered me to bed,
Once it was a relief to wake from nightmares
And see the slow child's face of the clock.
That face is no longer innocent, it is all our deaths.
Living is hard work.
I punch in and punch out,
Paid the minimum wage
Even in disappointments,
Eager for some 5 o'clock that never comes.

If mornings have become more difficult,
Evenings have become impossible.
God comes out of his room
Winding an alarm clock
To say goodnight, asking the time,
Saying, "Synchronize clocks,
Let them all be wrong in unison."

A JIG FOR MY WAKE

I wore loud ties bought for
50 cents in thrift shops on
Flatbush Avenue in Brooklyn loved
Women from any safe distance
Lived in a suburb
Rode terrified motorcycles
Loved the abyss walked
On the grills over subways wrote
Poems loved drink from no distance
At all and lovely Irish reels

Play your tin whistles your pipes and your bones
Sing those songs I wrote for your voices of bourbon
Bury me in a suburb with my face in the rain
Under a stolen subway grill with my
Wrecked Triumph to carry me up the Flatbush
Avenues of another world
Let your women fish like boys with gum to bait
The pennies on my eyes:
Bury me in a loud tie.

I FIND MY FRIENDS

I find my friends in my own gestures,
even if many of them are otherwise lost to me.
Gerry's pouting smile and that wave of the
left hand that refuses to pay for anything
as he always refused to pay in anything worth
more than money. Jackson's arm encircling
and cradling his own head while he listened to music,
as if the sound were an axe and he was afraid
of losing his head to its invisible blade.
Becker's sly grin. Roland's great hands clap slowly
in my own when I find that rare performance worth
applause. Leticia sank into my arms as if I were the sea.
Like Mitch I arrive at parties early and leave late.
Like Alan I gesture freely at the blind telephone.
Like Diane I have learned to listen in silence.
Like Richard I am not afraid to touch
anyone who seems to need tenderness. I am afraid
to need tenderness; however, like Monica, I am more
afraid of not being able to return it.
There are many others.
Tonight, listening
to Nick play, I found myself with my head cradled
    in my own arms,
lips pursed in a sly smile, wanting to applaud slowly
and loudly yet sitting in silence, loving that
silly face in the mirror of the window across
from my seat, knowing that I am loved and loving the
old friends I find buried in my body, loving
the self I am becoming, knowing how all
these other arms still wait for me.

THE WOMAN WHO LOVES
THE 18TH CENTURY

*Human life is everywhere a state in which much is to be
endured, and little to be enjoyed.*
                                                    – Samuel Johnson

She has the eyes of a child waking after
    general anesthesia.
Otherwise her face shows no evidence of breakage.
She is grateful a face can be reassembled now more
    invisibly than those
Blue willow plates her husband shattered against
    a kitchen wall.

Perfectly beautiful in the web of her new fragility,
    she ties words
One-handed into surgeons' knots. I want to touch the
Scars I cannot see. She knows Addison, Pope,
    and Swift like
Their shared mistress. A court order keeps her
    husband ten city blocks away.

Still, she wears his ring, I am afraid, and my
    long schedule
Of departures has no allowance for a woman
    in the wrong
Century. She thinks *Rasselas* saves souls. I can't agree.
Later she weeps as if bleeding to death through
    her eyes.

THE WOMAN WHO LOVES
THE 18TH CENTURY

Last night I left the hospital early and walked down
    to the college
To hear Tom Wolfe rave about a past I understood
    only when it was the present.
An old lover standing by the door said hello as I left.
    I couldn't
Remember her name. I wanted to ask how Dublin
    had been.

This morning I read *Rasselas* on the long ride
    to the clinic.
Today, perhaps, the children I care for smiled at
    me more.
This evening, in a Metro station in downtown
    Washington, mortality
Tapped me on the shoulder like an old lover
    I'd forgotten.

Tomorrow I'll read Swift.

ELEGY FOR ROBERT CHAMBERLAIN

You know how it freaks me out when people
    break appointments.
Bobby, I was going to be in San Francisco in the
    middle of June.
We were going to go sailing. I had it all planned.
    I knew you were sick.
Why did you die? You were forty the year I was born
But you kept getting younger.
We were nearly the same age the last time I saw you.
We were going to have some good times.
You knew my whole family. They leaned on you
    and you leaned back.
Bobby, I was never one of the crummy relatives.
I knew you were sick. Why did you leave me?
You and I were in love with the same woman.
    My cousin,
She made me meet you. I was shy;
She knew nothing was enough, yet one does what
    one can.
I talked to June on the phone every week. I gave
    her advice.
She is not angry but is grieving. You used to ask
    about me.
She'd read you poems I sent, and you enjoyed them
More with the morphine than without. Not many
    have such an audience.
Didn't you want to stay and hear more? There's
    no excuse

For what you did to us. Even your nurses were in
    love with you.
You were going to introduce me to the redhead. She
    liked me already.
Only one more month. Why couldn't you wait?
You wore a beautiful suit to take me to dinner
    in ragged jeans and acne.
You cared about everything. You had responsibilities.
You did everything well except living forever. Jonny
    left for North Dakota.
She said nothing and the phone went unanswered.
    I kept sending poems,
With witty little notes. My mother called from
    Montana today
To tell me you were dead. I have cried my way
    through half a roll
Of pink toilet paper tonight. I think of you grinning
    around your
Fantastic nose, you handsome devil. Do you think
    it's going to be
That much fun here without you? You could drive
    a truck through
The hole you've made in our lives. I imagine you
    doing that, as a
Joke. If you think it's funny, wait until we realize
    you are gone.

DEAR MONICA

Perhaps this will be the last letter.
I know I want you to remember me as I will
    remember you.
Here I am again, sitting on the back porch
As summer begins, writing for you as I have
    so often written
For no one but you.
A neighbor's roses the color of your hair stand in a
Mason jar on my physics textbook, the optics chapter
Bookmarked with a raven's feather you sent last year.

Sometimes I know I am still alive.
Whenever this happens I think of you
And wish you the love you need and the love you
    can give.
You have given me more than you can suspect.

I remember another porch, an evening in the
Early summer, a house built on a
Virginia hill just before Mr. Jefferson's War.
The dark was falling like a light rain into the warmth
Of the valley below. A mare and her foal
Played running games in their round paddock.
Other horses breathed and sighed in the stables.
The first fireflies began to signal their dark mistresses
As the sun just touched the last waves of the
    Blue Ridge.
That dark bowl of a valley with its
    changing constellations
Was a sky we could understand.   Even the old light

Of the stars will not go on forever. I thought of you
Then, as I think of you now. I was happy,
And you were beautiful, swimming toward me,
I thought, through
The ice-cream headache rivers of your faraway Maine.
I wrote a letter.

Why were we never lovers? You were merciful.
You knew this would happen.
Already there had been six months I tried not
      to think of you,
But heard your name in my voice
So many times I wrote again.
You too have tried to say goodbye and failed.

Such failures make us live. I remember your anger,
How you taught me. I remember why tears swam
      in my eyes like fish
As you moved through the waters of a death
You could finally remember.
You taught me your answers.
Now I can ask again,
Now I can fail.

Roland writes from New York,
A long gossipy letter
With a buried, too casual mention –
Monica finally fell for some guy.
I always hoped love might be possible,
And now I know.
                          Not much news from here:
Still studying rainbows and stealing roses.

PARABLE OF THE BAD SHEPHERD

When I rode down Cemetery Road thirty years ago
   at dusk,
After a matinee of *The Blob* at the Varsity Theater,
I knew they were there, held down under the feet of the
Live oaks and the man-eating stones.
Pretending to be late and hungry
I pedaled faster, the wind at my back.
This was a small town when I was small.
Among its citizens, only the dead were strangers,
Easily forgotten before dinner.

Forgetting is harder now.
Riding a borrowed bicycle, in no hurry,
I turn left onto a street meant for processions
And stop at the chapel office
Clutching a sweaty bouquet of daisies.
I stare at a limp copy of *Newsweek*
While I wait my turn to see the man
Selling two women adjoining plots.

The cemetery at Davis, California,
Looks like a golf course.
Almond orchards I remember to the
South have been uprooted and groomed
Into undulating lawns.
An intermittent rainbow floats in the spray
Of automatic sprinklers.
The groundskeeper speaks of the weather
Then is silent with me as we walk to the flat markers
I could not have found by myself.

Once a month for years I've seen her distant ghost
On the street or in the subway
Turn into some other tall woman with long hair
    the color of honey
Who has nothing to say to me.
I've come three thousand miles hoping not to find
    her grave.

She is buried in the old, rough part of the cemetery
On the side of the trees that must catch the morning sun,
Beside her sister and her sister's boy.
The litter of cut flowers seasoned by light
And the hard municipal water,
The same final date cut into these three stones,
Could punctuate some local tragedy of wreck or fire:

It was no accident, but a mistake I tried to make.
Jim Jones was the only man I ever met whose face
    gave off light.
I envied his flock their Technicolor shepherd,
The valley he promised the bombs wouldn't reach,
Their digestible religion with all the gods winnowed out.

I needed a teacher but he didn't want me.
He wanted the woman I would marry and both
    her sisters,
Angels of the lost poor, miraculous with children.
He told me I was on another path,
Had a lot of people I had to tell goodbye
I might never see again.
He could see the future and I wasn't in it.
I was hitch-hiking north

On a whim with two weeks to spare
Before induction. I thought I'd have
To be lucky to reach Montana,
Where all my grandparents were gathered,
The living and the dead,
So had told no one of my plans.

Jones was wrong about never seeing them again.
Death was more common than acne among the medics,
But I was careful, reported dead only once.
I always marched anonymously among the riflemen.

In San Francisco the last year of her life
I called Peoples Temple and left a message.
Visiting medical students could stay free
In the Hansen's Disease housing, war-surplus
Barracks at Marine Hospital.
I was in the right place, the family leper
Carrying the bacillus of divorce.
The noseless woman down the hall
Kept the only phone busy with her bleating Spanish.
I'll never know if Annie tried to return my call.

A thousand people, many poor and black,
Many others who had chosen not to be rich,
Fled with Jones to Guyana, pursued, they said,
By their persecutors. Cornered,
Despairing in the world, the sheep lay down their lives
For their shepherd. The report she died by gunfire,
Not Kool-Aid laced with poison, is an odd source
    of comfort:
I won't leave these flowers on a stranger's grave.

THE FIRST YEAR MY EARNINGS
WILL EXCEED MY FATHER'S

My father is working only for himself now. He is
    building a place to die.
For the second time he has come back too late to the
    old place.
Collect calls from a phone booth on a highway answer
    my desperation
With orders to read Luke, that's straight stuff. Luke
    is at least
Himself, I am myself, and you, you are no longer
    yourself.
What happened to that godless drunk who took his
    speechless son
On cruises through the alcoholic haze in search of
    gangs of black men
They might fight together but could never find?
    Nine hours in a
Drunk tank changed your life, my scientist.
    You found, somehow,
The calculus which had eluded you: Matthew, Mark,
    Acts and Numbers.
You had half a roof up when winter came to your
    father's land.
I'll send a check but cannot agree to trust in God.
    My gentle father,
Who taught me well how not to drink
Who are you now to teach me not to think?

ICU

The electrical activity of the heart
of a man who was alive yesterday
is legible to me now,
written on graph paper
in a language it has
taken me ten years to learn.

A spear pierced the left side
of his last good dream
and he never truly woke.

XMAS IN BROOKLYN, 1982

The news is bad tonight,
So I listen to music, instead.
It seems odd to be happy.
Pilgrims and troops crowd Bethlehem
As usual, short of hotel rooms.
Children continue dying on
Television whether I watch or not.
History is malignant and repetitious.

When I left the hospital today
Just before visiting hours began,
The seasonal platoon of stuffed animals
Already stood guard at the entrance,
Larger and more colorful than life.
A dark entrepreneur in a shabby coat
Moved among them, brushing snow
From their faces. Hand lettered
Price tags fluttered like
Small, complicated flags.

There are no toy stores among those miles
Of tenements rocked blind, burned, then abandoned
As if the next war had come early but couldn't stay.
I saw a patient's mother across the street
On my long walk to the subway.
Like conspirators we smiled slightly but we did
    not wave.

By morning the stuffed animals will be gone.
I may see a few again on my ward,
Last-minute gifts guarding the beds
Of children who will never get well.
There is only one war:
Stuffed animals on one side,
History on the other.

EPITHALAMION

for Ned and Alice

Rain falls, gathers into rivers,
Flows to the sea carrying its salt.
Love is inevitable, silent as water –
If we are patient it will come to us.
The islands rise up out of the old rain
To give us a place to wait.

I have watched and waited with you,
Have seen the moon from Oahu,
Your faces in the moon.
How long your journey has been
Toward each other, back and forth
Through continents, through lovers,
Through years of your lives and your own hopes.

No rain fell in the desert of your separations,
But hope is a cactus, and your friends were
Birds flying between you,
Reminding you it was the same sky,
Carrying the white message of wings.

No one can say the way half of us bleed
Is an accident. The moon skidded somehow
    from the womb
Of the sea; the continents slipped
Away from each other and are still traveling.

Past the full moon you have finally seen
Each other's faces; the separate roads
You have traveled so long have come together,
Where the cactus promises to flower at last.

THE PAIN

I had a patient once who knew one phrase.
Falling down drunk in the street, or just falling,
he broke up every cast we put on him
    and never healed.
Finally I admitted him from the emergency room
to stretch his shattered leg in traction
and hear him cry "the pain, the pain,"
two months last year.

Such patients go by different names
in different places, but they are all the same.
They wait until they're dying
and then brought in by cops they smell
like nothing I ever knew before, some mix of
excrement and teargas. They cannot bear
the wait that goes with being poor,
they've learned the dying never wait.
So, at midnight, you smell them coming.
Even the cops puke sometimes.
Even the tiled room with the hose
leaves them stinking and infested.

They are today's edition of
the battered textbooks of disease
I left behind three years ago,
and every day I leave behind
a new edition of myself. At three in the morning
a cop tells me over a plastic cup of bad coffee
"they're good for only one thing,
teaching us our jobs."
We almost care for them,
practice until we get it right,
and then we move uptown.

I almost care for them;
they hurt me when they can.
It hurts me that I always hurt them back.
I have stopped an elevator between floors
to scream like a man caught in a car wreck
after working thirty hours straight and found it did
     no good,
the loudspeakers cry my name. There is a man
stinking of blood, oil and beer waiting for
another pair of hands in the emergency room
and he cannot stop screaming.

I have seen a battered intern bend to blunt
a needle on the floor to make a screaming patient feel it.
I have broken a woman's ribs
to squeeze blood from her heart into her brain,
and kissed dead men until my lips were numb.
I have burned holes in white jackets and my own skin
with the cancer-killing poisons the nurses will not give,
poisons I have pumped into veins until the
    veins collapsed,
have watched patients who could talk and smile
turn into plants I water like a gardener.

I've seen babies born addicted to addicted mothers
scream when their faces show
and seem to want to crawl back in against
the punishing contractions of the womb
as if they knew they faced two months of
weaning from the needle their unknown mothers loved.
I have cut flesh with no remorse and no anesthesia
to let a baby out, and thought abortion was a sacrament.

I have seen children with every bone broken, healed,
half healed and fresh that day, seen skin marked with
the loops of convenient appliance cords, seen a face
branded with the prow of a hot iron.
I have touched, gently as the antennae of a roach,
a violated two-year-old who screamed at everything,
even her own hands groping toward tattered flesh.
I have diagnosed gonorrhea in nonchalant four-year-olds,
accepted gratefully the thanks for
what touch I had from an eight-year-old
ripped open as if she'd given birth
to the uncle who raped her. Once, across the hall
from pain like that, a five-year-old girl
sang all of "Silent Night" to me,
sitting on my examining table swinging
her small, perfect legs as I did not weep.

I have kept the dying alive not because I love life
but because I hate an empty bed, something the
emergency room can always fill with another of
    the dying.
Sometimes they come up with no bed free
and they die in the halls.
Sometimes they die at home suddenly with the children
who play innocently with the body for hours.

I have slept five nights a week for years,
yet they have something left to teach me,
and even if I learn everything I need to leave,
and leave them, still at night sometimes when I have
    no sleep
to spare, I will wake and cry, "the pain, the pain."

LEARNING THE LANGUAGE

I.

The Salvadorans say "If you won't let us live
In our own country, we'll live in yours."

They say there is a kind of earthquake that
Shakes you out of bed and drops the roof on your
Family, leaves you alone stumbling through rubble
On solid ground again. You can rebuild
Beside strangers who will become friends,
Who will smile when you can talk of the lost.

They say war is another kind of earthquake, worse,
The real earthquake, the one that has lasted years.
They say your friends and family die and disappear
Until there are too many of the lost to remember.

This real earthquake can dump bodies
In open fields to attract the women who will search
Methodically, but very quickly, for faces
They love before the sun can mutilate them.

This real earthquake can reach into your house,
Bind your son with wire in front of you, cut off
His genitals and stuff the organs into his mouth,
Only his eyes asking "Why did you make me live?"

II.

Some houses have no doors. Dark faces float by
On a river of bodies in worn, too colorful clothing.
English is not spoken here.

Feral dogs hunt rats through vacant lots.
Uniformed in mutilation, each beggar patrols a corner.
Homeless children die of incurable diseases,
Mothers sell themselves in the street,
Cops turn away, paid not to see.

The part of Central America where I work as a doctor
Is six stops into Brooklyn on the J Train.

Three years ago I spoke Spanish
Only well enough to ask about pain.
Now I am beginning to understand the answers:
This is where the real earthquake began,
This is where it will end.

EATING LEFTOVERS ON NANTUCKET

On Sunday mornings in the summer,
Quakers sitting in their gathered silence on
Fair Street can hear the hymns of
Episcopalians down on Centre,
Across the slanted cobbles of Main.

Bumblebees among the daylilies
Sound like distant sermons from the front porch
Of the house on North Star Lane,
Where the three of us, friends and family now
    twenty years,
Sit together rocking, not saying much, and the empty
Rocker I bought for my wife keeps time with us on
    the teak decking.

The people who named this island said
"No one can get rich if he treats his family right;"
But I am well-treated, never the poor uncle –
Even if Liz is just over the horizon on the Cape
Vacationing with her lover, another woman.

My nephew offers me a job as his next au pair
Then holds my hand as we walk away from the sea.
I've been promoted, after years of struggle,
From dishwasher to sous chef under the orders of
My eleven year-old princess niece.

She and I bake the same cake twice from scratch
To get it right, and the family eats
Every crumb of both golden cakes.
Grilled fresh tuna shows up the next day
In sandwiches on Portuguese bread.

Four days after I sliced them thin for burgers,
Mark sautés the red onions
Into a big goodbye frittata
With yesterday's roast new potatoes,
Triumphant to be using up every egg as well.

Last inches of wine go into this sauce and that,
And all the egg whites saved from the two cakes
Come out of the Aga as sugary, long-baked meringues.
It's true that leftovers taste better everywhere.
                                        Even at home
WASPs singing gospel sound sweeter three
    blocks away.

THE SOUND OF AIR OVER WINGS
(7 Sonoma Haiku)

1.

Arm-shaped oak reaches
Out from Two Rock Valley floor –
Hawk lands on its hand.

2.

Blackbirds feed under
The hooves of the dark horses –
Walk away, then fly.

3.

Flash in roadside grass –
Obsidian arrowhead,
Or fresh raven shit?

4.

Cumulonimbic
Vulture vortex, vanishes –
Something's not moving.

5.
Last breath in strobe lights —
Only one EMT sees
The tattooed Angel.

6.
Hummingbird hovering
Outside the dojo window —
Inside we're blooming.

7.
On the long flight East
Trying to write this haiku —
My pen exploded.

FIVE TASKS TAUGHT BY HOSPICE NURSES
to my brother

1. *Say Goodbye*

You called me at work to ask for a loan
And said goodbye as sweetly as if I'd said yes.
I was unhappy, and probably rude.
It was the last time we talked.

2. *Express Forgiveness*

I forgive you for stepping over the edge,
Wearing a roofer's safety harness
Clipped stylishly to nothing,
Momentary angel over Arizona.

When you were seven
You flew the swing set outside
Our Chilean house through an earthquake
As walls and ceilings collapsed into themselves.
"More, make it do that again!"

Your life was not as short as I feared
Nor as long as I hoped.

3. *Request Forgiveness*

Forgive me for not lending you the money
To buy that motorcycle,
For not admiring your poetry,
For never taking a photograph of you with my sons.
Forgive me for not wrestling with you into more
Sunsets the summer before I was drafted.

Forgive me for being your imitation angel,
For leaving you with that elephant in the living room.
Forgive me for living.

4. *Affirm Affection*

I love you
For being obvious about loving me
When I was fifteen and
Thought I couldn't bear to be loved.
You were too young to know better.
You were so alive,
Your death seemed impossible –
If you could die everyone would.

5. *Express Gratitude*

Thank you for giving me back
My lost family and Montana,
Where we scattered your ashes
According to your instructions:
Up Big Creek Canyon
And on the hundred-year
Flood plain of the Bitterroot.
West Yellowstone burned all the week
Of your death, frosting windshields white in July.
Now, when I visit – and I visit often – I do work I love,
While I stay in a lodge built ten years ago
Of first-growth timber
Salvaged from that fire.

Now I see: living is a kind of slow burning,
And love is what we salvage from the fire.

MEDITATION LESSON IN THE *PAYS d'OC*

I'll close my eyes on the blue hills
across rock-bound vineyards
through a screen of olive trees
over hedges of rosemary and lavender,
paying attention to my breath.

Fragrance, memory, birdsong,
the clamor of cicadas—I notice these
then return my attention to my breath.

The slow caress of the sun
moves over my face just as it moves over
vineyards, ripening grapes into the blood of stones.

Paying attention only to my breath
I inhale something big and alive.
Instead of dying I cough up a butterfly, watch it
dry its wings in the sun to rejoin the iridescent cloud
floating on the scent of lavender.

Pay attention to your breath, telling you
this world is a place full of trapdoors
hinged subtly as a lepidopteran wing.
Pay attention only to your breath.

MILLENNIUM FIRE

Surgical masks my sons wore
Picking chokecherries in the woods this morning
Are marked with the gray shadows
Of lips forming prayers.

We risk arrest to swim in the Bitterroot River
Where the smoke reminds us constantly,
Like an angry Bodhisattva:
We are still breathing.
Cars with headlights on at noon
Pass by on 93 in an endless funeral procession:
The sun confuses itself with the full moon.

Debris columns from drought-fed
Fires no one is fighting
Hold up the brown roof of the sky.
From my mother's porch, Mount St. Mary
Appears and disappears,
Outlined in a light that breathes in wind
And exhales clouds.

For a moment a fire among the trees
Across two miles of canyon
Might be autumn
In New England, if autumn could
Outrun deer and melt steel.
Dark men are dancing ceaselessly for rain:
We don't know how to pray —
So are praying to learn.

THREE FROM UPAYA ZEN CENTER

Early Sitting

Not crickets singing
But choral borborygmi —
Bellies full of light.

Walking Meditation

Priestly hands flutter
An order to Dr. Darth —
Quieten your breath.

Zen Spider

Trapped in the sink
Two days before her escape —
By TP staircase.

GRIEF WORK

Weeks after the funeral
Only one pair of sparrows
Puzzled over dooryard snow
Blank after sixty years of crumbs.

I was done talking,
Done feeding those flocks of birds with *him* gone,
Done tolerating a kitchen full of visitors
Expressing sympathy for the loss
I thought of as desertion:
Next stop – nursing home.

That pretty hospice volunteer mixed
Warm water, yeast and flour before
I threw *her* out –
But I kept the fragrant dough
She left rising beside the woodstove,
To knead, and slash, and beat it
Gray as stones –
Unfit for human consumption.

Over-salted as it was
By sweat and tears,
I baked it anyway.

Too hard to cut,
The flat loaf shatters
Under my husband's hammer,
I pound shards to dusty chunks
Sweep it all up in my apron,
And scatter the whole mess
Into the swirl
Of all those returning, vigilant birds.

DYING FOR BEGINNERS

to Wes Burwell, D. Min.

I.

Our chaplain's sixtieth birthday present to himself
was the new career he saw on a vision-fast in
    the canyon lands.
He would help others over the river, as harbor seals
are said to help lost swimmers, nudging them
    toward shore –
practice for mortality by serving other mortals.

II.

Hospice staff struggled with the daughter who declined
    to tell
her demented, dying mother of a son's unexpected death.
Then the old lady saw her boy waiting for her to cross,
thought the chaplain might know a little prayer to help
her find her ticket for the ferry; and he did.

III.

The engineer with end stage cancer lived for their visits,
not only meandering with the chaplain through
    memories –
his loving marriage, work well done, well-educated
    children –
he prized the weekly chance to scoff at angels and any
    possibility of heaven.

                His last word? "Wow!"

IV.

When Silas had his fifth MI we put Nan safely in the
    nursing home again,
Where her slow-moving ALS would have left her
    forever years ago
without his constant vigilance.
The transfer had become routine.
                  The night Silas died in the ICU
in spite of pressors, ventilation, ICD and CPR —
the stream of alphabetic torment he'd carefully
    directed in advance —
I called ahead so Nan's hair could be brushed while
    Wes held her hand
and I raced the small-town news to her bedside.
A unit clerk put me on hold for a few measures
    of Pachelbel,
returned to tell me not to make the twenty-minute
    drive.
Her nurse just found her lifeless and could
    pronounce her,
if I would certify that death had been expected.

V.

A circle of a hundred mourners standing in a
    California meadow
released their helium balloons into a flood of sunlight.
The ring of rising multicolored dots was bent by
    currents of the breeze
into the kind of lopsided heart a child might have
    drawn for reassurance

against the blank, untouchable sky.

MEMORIAL DAY

Fishing the oxbows of the Lamprey River
With my sons is how we can revisit my father
Closer than the Bitterroot, where we scattered
    his ashes.

Gabriel, himself tossed back by the Angel of Death
Just a week ago, is no longer grateful
Simply to be able to swallow:

He wants the mosquitoes to stop biting
And the trout to start. Jacob catches
One freshwater mussel and two trees,

A white pine and a hemlock. He claims
Both are too small to keep.
Uncle Cookie lands a six-incher,

And extracts the hook as carefully as the surgeon
Backed the Mylar Star of David out of
Gabriel's distal esophagus last Sunday night.

Cookie holds the stunned fish upright in the water
Until it can flash from his hand like a knife.
Catch and release is the story of my life, of all
    our lives:

But a Titleist winks up at me from the moss-black
Granite of the river bottom, ten miles
Upstream from the nearest country club,

Like a jokey message from the old man
Who taught six grandsons how to fish
And how to judge a lie. He claims

He's all right after all. It wasn't hell he smelled
As he was dying, it was my lost brother Michael,
On the other side, firing up the grill for trout.

AFTERWORD: Origins of the Earwax Patrol

The patient I'll call Miss Cooper sat with the other elderly people in wheelchairs and imitation Barcaloungers surrounding the island of the nursing station most of the day, leaning on each other, interpreting, watching, and, of course, being watched. It was where the action was. Miss Cooper still corrected polite staff members who assumed she had been married. She hadn't, but she would show you a painting of the school in Vermont named after her, if you knew to ask.

The picture hung over her bed. She spent as little time there as possible. "Afraid I won't wake up," she said. She'd outlasted two roommates when she started failing herself. Miss Cooper followed the usual trajectory of Alzheimer's, becoming uninterested in the halting conversations that helped pass the time in the nursing home, eating less, losing weight. Boredom can be the real plague in such places, as Bill Thomas says, along with loneliness and helplessness. When Miss Cooper became bed bound and mute, signifying a life expectancy of six months or less in her disease, the charge nurse called in a hospice referral extracted from an exasperated physician. This was five or ten years ago, before most people really understood that Alzheimer's is a terminal illness.

The charge nurse wanted Miss Cooper to get some extra attention as she was dying. At the time, the Medicare regulations governing chronic nursing home care stipulated an hour of one-on-one care out of twenty-four — not enough even when you're not dying. The nurse had worked twenty years in and out of nursing homes and saw hospice people as quiet, competent, and collaborative. She knew that you could talk to them about death without scaring them, and they liked parties too. They'd move a birthday party up if someone was dying too fast to make it to the "real" date. More important, they would be there a lot more than an hour a day, and they'd pay attention. Hospice volunteers or nursing aides would sit with Miss Cooper and talk about her school as she approached death, or sing, or just be quietly present. Some of them had beautiful voices.

The hospice nurse who evaluated Miss Cooper worried about a bedsore that started developing on her left heel. I was asked in to take a look when it grew bigger in spite of treatment, as her own doctor was not scheduled to visit the nursing home for a number of weeks. "Likely she's just starting to shut down," the hospice nurse said. "Nothing else has changed." Hospice clinicians know that a decubitus ulcer developing suddenly and spontaneously can be a signal that a person had started to die. Signing up for care by my hospice signs you up for a medical director's visit, or associate medical director's visit in my case. Luke Hill was the medical director then.

I went in and talked with the nursing staff, heard Miss Cooper's story, and measured the ulcer accurately with a millimeter ruler so I'd be able to tell if it continued to grow. Luke taught me that a more general routine physical exam should be part of all patient visits – I can hear him saying, gruffly, "You never know what you'll find." I took my Welch Allyn otoscope out of my black bag and opened the battery compartment to take out a reversed AA battery, reinserted it to allow power to get to the halogen bulb. If you don't keep batteries reversed in those instruments they tend to turn themselves on in your black bag. Good luck begging new batteries from a skeptical RN.

An ear exam is a small thing and takes only a moment. Under most circumstances the human ear is a self-cleaning mechanism. But with inactivity and age, perhaps with the added bad luck of having an hourglass-shaped ear canal, earwax tends to accumulate. You have to look for it. Miss Cooper had more earwax than I had ever seen in one person. I could see the wax without the otoscope; using the instrument and holding each ear grasped above and behind the lobe to straighten out the canal I could
see it went all the way back to her eardrums on
both sides.

There was a moment of temptation. I had another patient to see and I was going to be late for dinner again. It looked like quite an undertaking. At least I could get started. In the end it took a week of alternating treatments, doing a little at a time, to get enough wax out to be able to see the eardrum. We used everything: a water-pick, ear candles. In the end the peroxide soaks did the trick. She started reacting to my arrival after the third or fourth visit, quite displeased to have me pulling her ear this way and that, washing her ears out with a syringe filled with a body-temperature peroxide, water and gentle detergent solution. When I finished I wrote the orders that would keep the wax from accumulating again, something a physician patient taught me. Two drops of 3% peroxide once a week will keep most people's eardrums clear. I really didn't expect her to live long enough to benefit from that.

But by the next week Miss Cooper had taken her place at the nursing station again, was speaking, listening, and eating. She gained weight, her decubitus healed, and she was generally improved enough to consider discharging her from hospice for becoming too healthy, what we called "failure to fail." She was still alive and chattering away a year later, off the hospice service. Since that experience I have always carried an otoscope to house calls as well as nursing home visits. Some of the hospice nurses have sardonically taken to calling my consultation rounds "the earwax patrol," in honor of my obsession with otoscopy. It's true that an ear exam is a small thing; we cannot all do great things, as Mother Theresa said, but we can all do small things with great love.